RUN.

poems by

Sara Youngblood Gregory

Finishing Line Press
Georgetown, Kentucky

RUN.

Copyright © 2022 by Sara Youngblood Gregory
ISBN 978-1-64662-952-7 First Edition
All rights reserved under International and Pan-American Copyright Conventions. No part of this book may be reproduced in any manner whatsoever without written permission from the publisher, except in the case of brief quotations embodied in critical articles and reviews.

ACKNOWLEDGMENTS

"you say my name" and "drop the bomb or help me means the same thing to the fbi" were originally published in *The Broadkill Review*
"climate death but my blood runs hot" was originally published in *Queen Mob's Tea House*

There are so many people to which I owe my endless love and gratitude:

Julie R. Enszer, my friend and mentor, for first inviting me into the world of lesbian-feminist writing and publishing.

Vi Khi Nao, a brilliant poet and mentor, for guiding me through many, many manuscripts with grace and enthusiasm.

My Oxygente friends Martha Addy-Young, Jay Brecker, Brian Cochran, Bonnie Naradzay, Juan Palomo, Cintia Santana, Linda Stryker, and Susan Wheatley for tending my work and watering my confidence.

Christen Kincaid, my editor, and all the wonderful folks at Finishing Line Press. Mom, Dad, and Emma, for who I am and who I am not.

Rachel Komich, for being my best friend and my always-first reader.

And finally, thank you to my fiancé, Salomé Grasland, for designing RUN.'s front cover. For the support and love that keeps me walking. For being the eye and the storm.

Publisher: Leah Huete de Maines
Editor: Christen Kincaid
Cover Art: Salomé Grasland
Author Photo: Salomé Grasland
Cover Design: Elizabeth Maines McCleavy

Order online: www.finishinglinepress.com
also available on amazon.com

Author inquiries and mail orders:
Finishing Line Press
PO Box 1626
Georgetown, Kentucky 40324
USA

Table of Contents

august 1

Ichetucknee or How the Color Red Can't Live Underwater 3

Remember When You Were Selling Your Plasma? 5

A Series Called Byline (Obit) 7

My Aunt Reads Me The Personal Ad for Lot's Wife, Age 5 8

Self-portrait 9

At night, when we think the other is sleeping. 10

You as Noon 12

On How Mosquitos Are Locked Doors 13

Song for Wife, Unborn 14

Song for Wife, Unexpected 15

climate death but my blood runs hot 16

drop the bomb or help me means the same thing to the fbi 17

you say my name 19

The Rich Are Only Defeated When Running for Their Lives 20

Election Eve 2020 21

august

                        it was august

                        long and heavy

crammed into a

house   of   three

barely   women

blowing off steam

and   into   my

mouth   a   jay

screams,

                             forget

                        it was years of fire

                        an elected fire

electric under the

sky I run in the

arms of   barely

talking

of   burning and

watching   memory

revise us

make a cup out of water let us be t he last to know

Ichetucknee or How the Color Red Can't Live Underwater

we go

and I can't help but

                                                  swallow

            at least one fish dream

            look across and sing back

there's a 40 foot cave and

red can't travel more than 10

                So your skin drains creamy

                    the further you go   cold

                can sometimes make ghosts

                      out of lovers

in the winter

        you buy a truck I can't get into hold

        my waist I jump / follow / dive

              you down the cave

                                                  touch hesitant

the sand waving at you   waving back

   at the lover looking Blue.

there is a perfect circle where fresh water meets teeth.

Remember When You Were Selling Your Plasma?

                        Every 30 miles is a dead deer

           Remember when you were selling your plasma

            how every workers comp letter made you cry

Or the cardboard burning on the night of the meteor

    shower then, later, squatting in the cold with the

bucket of boiled water? You combed my hair with your

                  fingers.

    I started smoking that summer, then

    reluctantly winter. I learned to breathe

        menthols down to the nub

              then wear the filter around my neck, or

                    my ears sometimes, too.

I nibble in times of crisis   yank   it's the idea that

    I'm choosing something bad

            but not as bad as it could be.

        Remember when you counted your addictions

on two hands? You said I was still safe, I had more fingers than you by a lot. When I see the high voltage fence across the field

I wonder.

A Series Called Byline (Obit)

A hand when it holds a hand is still empty. The city in the sky is just a star. Elon Musk is building a colony on mars. by the time I'm 30 she'll be as big as New York & empty. I see the news flash   NEWS   N E W S   N E W S   N E W S   It's a big deal to pay $139 to get your passport updated from country to planet of origin. I'm thinking about my check, my $600 which keeps my lover from selling their blood again. Plasma sh ipped to stimmy the cells in Elon's hands. I turn on the tap. Fill the pot til she's heavy. Wat ch the water boil on low. I hear there's no getting old up there. The blood has a barcode.

My Aunt Reads Me the Personal Ad for Lot's Wife, Age 5

andro doll for
renegade top
as in aggregate
aggress or
obsessive ISO
caressive pro
gressive missus
minus switches
Home grown n
housebroken s
eeks accessible
pussy and / or
parking ready
for a tight fit
strang er void
with hair i am
the looking gl
ass spit in my
strip mall eve
meet sodom ie
me ....

Self-portrait

there's jasmine growing in the fence, finally

so strong you smell them over your own body

while caterpillars explode into moths

you watch one on the ground, frozen

ants on the grey wings, weighing her down

she struggles but can't fly away; there are too many

their mouths are so heavy

you ask *should I help her?*

but what you mean *dare I play god?*

that's the kind of person you are

you watch until it's too late

At night, when we think the other is sleeping.

I eat. You drink.

***

I lay outside the trailer-turned-altar. It's the second truly hot day of spring. I'm on your favorite blanket in the grass. You sit on the steps, bending down but still looking up. I'm smoking and you're crying.

***

You are the loneliest god ever.

The blanket is dirty and so soft. I

am the fanatic at your feet.

***

Our agreement is simple: I buy the trailer. You buy the truck. One isn't much use without the other, which is how we like it.

***

I'm not going to be one of those paranoid lovers. I can't.

I know.

***

Addiction is really no one's goddamn business. There is nothing immortal about getting fucked up.

***

There is stinging on my legs, thighs, neck. The blanket is on the bed. The bed is swarming with ants. I wake up. I wake you up. We shake out the covers. *Don't turn on the light.* My voice running low. *We don't want to see what we can feel.*

***

A body is god-stolen. Self-ordained. A beast at the straw cradle.

You as Noon

a patch of afternoon where a cat sleeps

On a red floor   you   a window

unlock chipped paint sticking to the glass

you open   you unlocked   you

on T with the best look in your eye   you

during heartbreak   suicidal from your first

not you moment   you   the strange noon

in the woods just settling in   consider that

you are never   and always   doing fine

Consider i am here and there that i am for   you

there is nothing as short   as the way home

On How Mosquitos Are Locked Doors

like a missing tooth

i run my tongue over the spot where you again

again gone   the way the key slides

sticking jiggling

        feeling the   yes right there of a popped lock

open tooth   we kept separate rooms shared a fridge

not food   there was one key between us

i wake up to a wide open house   you hated

the way I swept the summer heat swung open

the windows I'd sweat while I cooked   sweat to dye sheets

there is no breeze in that neighborhood   I insisted

        I invited   no one over

we flooded the sink the gravity bong it was fine

panic attack

        in the shower   after   again   I'd wake up

to an unlocked house

worse than can happen you gone what's the worst that could happen

mosquitos gather in the home you wake up in rashes   surprised

or how

their mouths too   are keys in the flesh

Song for Wife, Unborn
After Diane di Prima

Lover

when i am done with anger

there will be the breaking

of what world we made and

burnt together   left alone

is the day

you stopped choosing me

leave what warmth in

the murder forest

covered by dust the bastard

love i bore you now,

away

Song for Wife, Unexpected
After Diane di Prima

Lover

you taught me

how broken hands

hold an eggshell love

Gentle   now

with what I give

there will be no taking back

climate death but my blood runs hot

the entire coast of southwest florida chokes herself out. red tide bloats the shore and i strip off my shirt stuff it under the door frame quick. we can smell the dead bodies through every crack the fish can't breathe and i can't cope. their bones are my earrings my dance card the silver spoon in my mouth mouth the words along with me *i love you from now til 2050*. my baby ties me between sheets forget the shore they say *i can't*. we have eighteen months until the end of all worth but queers have always lived like this. we are historically choked-out sea birds and i make nothing up. think aids in the eighties such heatwaves of july, nineteen eighty nine. my mother won't tell me if heatstroke killed my cousin jay or the sweating, gorgeous twinks who looked but never found. the government still won't speak our frothy, fag names; thirty years later they recall how death equals silence. they are killing us and by they i mean capitalists who blame us and by us i mean the birds and the fish the working poor the brown and the black and the angry and the the the. i am thirty before i realize how silence makes rainstorms out of dykes. how every one of our cousins turned red guts in a glass vase. the vice is everything jay birds never tell us of ourselves. you gasp from between my legs the only place safe to swim now and your mouth, dripping saltwater, red tide fingers, and my fish bone nipples. I don't make out the words.

drop the bomb or help me means the same thing to the fbi

my body is so wrecked with pain i walk like

    i'm 80 and arthritis is having a party

        mom is out out dancing and cuz no one retires

            anymore i head into work home office

                            creaking type type typing

                  garbage language into a garbage screen let
                        me lay my chest on your computer

                            getting messages like

                            baby i'll see you at lunch

            keep me clacking keep me from cracking

i get slack messages from HR saying i'm

paranoid i'm paranoid wrecked with

        pandemic.

                    When was the last time I said no?

                    no into her pillow. no into his hand.

                          no to overtime?

        my tongue and clack clack fingers and garbage

wreck body get sore from saying my own name: no

                    no no no

the fbi is tracking everything i do when i clack

most of which is to write garbage

which if translated to morse code is

/ drop the bomb or

help me /

which to the fbi means the same thing

paranoia that's fine pandemic is fine

as long as you're pretty

pain is starting to make me gaunt

in the way that looks like i've seen sunshine but

not felt it in years and years,

maybe since i was 21

what is left behind

i'm huffing petrichor and power lines in the

bathroom huffing whippets on weekends and

setting serotonin on fire this wednesday I am on

fire

you say my name

The only time you say my name
is when you are furious the hard
s is hot oil and smoke you push me
in the shopping cart at the end of the
world the shelves are empty you tell me accountability
is a deal breaker. Is it worth saying you leaving would
be the real panic? The shelves are empty
the cheap metal shoves into my shoulder
blades you tell me to stop being a brat
it stopped being cute last march.

The center of my 20s is housing instability
or maybe watching the world pandemic & is it
worth saying our first memory was 9/11?
the second is a cold swimming pool.

Now you just sound like my father he kicked
me out two months after we met then
exploded

you push me towards apocalypse with that word:
accountability. What am I supposed to do with a word I've
never felt? the shelves are empty and we're behind the glass
everyone in this central florida town
they run around us because there is no water
but so much candy

The rich are only defeated when running for their lives

The rich are only defeated when running for their lives

drop your ruling class dreams, your father's mansion

your finishing school (Harvard) was funded by the CIA

I saw Antigone at my private high school

Oedipus Rex and the sharp sharp hair pins

Feeling my first feeling

I watched Antigone die in that cave

noose rung like a bell

I go to gym class

each year my dad writes a letter

to the headmaster on why I deserve a scholarship

he packs my lunch every morning I learn to peel my own oranges

in a college dorm room I got a big payout after being hit by that first car

you were driving the Escalade so my life changed

I started catching up

Election Eve 2020
After Jenny Holzer

THE BLUE MOON IS UNDER THE TREE LINE FOR GOOD. THE WORST PASSES TOWARDS A NEW WEATHER / OPPRESSOR IT IS THE EVE OF A COLLECTIVE SHAM AN ELECTED MAN WHAT IS OLD MUST BE LAID TO DINE WHAT IS ELDER MUST BE MADE CHIPPED STONE. ISOLATE THE WHOLE FROM THE MANY, SOLIDARITY IS NOT UNITY BUT MORE SATISFYING IT IS THE MOST REAL WE CAN BE. IT IS THE EVE OF ELECTION 2020 I AM READING THE WRITING ON THE WALL. A RAPIST WILL LOSE THIS YEAR AND A RAPIST WILL WIN. BOTH HARKEN THE UNCOMMON. APOCALYPSE BLOOMS THERE WILL BE A FIRE LIKE NO OTHER.

With Thanks

Many, many poets influence my work. Here are just a few:

"Song for Wife, Unborn" and "Song for Wife, Unexpected" pay homage to Diane di Prima's "Song for Baby-O, Unborn."

"drop the bomb or help me means the same thing to the fbi" references linette reemnan's "The FBI Uses My Pronouns Correctly When They Search My Apartment For Evidence."

"The rich are only defeated when running for their lives" quotes from CLR James' *The Black Jacobin*.

"Election Eve 2020" pays homage to the Inflammatory Essays 1979–82 by Jenny Holzer.

Sara Youngblood Gregory is a lesbian writer and poet. As a journalist, her work on sexual wellbeing, disability, and queerness has appeared in *Vice, Cosmopolitan, TeenVogue, Huffington Post, Bustle, Dame Magazine, Bitch Media* and many others. Sara serves on the board of the lesbian literary and arts journal *Sinister Wisdom*, and recently served as co-editor of the forthcoming Trans/Feminism issue. Her non-fiction guide on navigating ethical nonmonogamy, *The Polyamory Workbook*, is out this fall.

As a poet, Sara has been nominated for Best of the Net, Best New Voices, and a Pushcart Prize. An alumni of *Kenyon Review* Writer's Workshop, you can find her work in places like Newfound Presss, Cream City Review, and Ghost City Press. *RUN.* is Sara's first chapbook.

You may also know Sara as sinister.spinster from Instagram, where they talk about kink, polyamory, and sex ed.

www.ingramcontent.com/pod-product-compliance
Lightning Source LLC
LaVergne TN
LVHW041524070426
835507LV00012B/1796